Discovering Natural Design

Kenneth Neville

Discovering Natural Design

MILLS & BOON LIMITED, LONDON

First published in Great Britain 1974 by
Mills & Boon Limited, 17–19 Foley Street,
London W1A 1DR.

© Kenneth Neville 1974

ISBN 0 263.05463.2

Book designed by Alec Davis
Made and Printed in Great Britain by
Butler & Tanner Ltd,
Frome and London.

Contents

Acknowledgements

My thanks to Mr Anthony Bury for his patience and skill in photographing my work for inclusion in this book. My thanks to Miss Brenda Simpson, Senior Lecturer in Movement Education, Charlotte Mason College of Education, Ambleside, and her students for the photograph of movement.

To my many friends and colleagues for their encouragement and constructive criticism.

Special thanks to my wife and family for their understanding and encouragement that made the writing of this book possible.

Introduction

There are many starting points for design. In this book I have outlined my own approach to creating design from natural forms in both two- and three-dimensional work. It is written in simple terms to provide readers who have no formal art training with a starting point for creating their own designs.

One cannot design in a vacuum. An awareness of line, form, texture, and colour is required and this can be achieved only through experience.

We have a readily available source of design in nature—we only need to stop, look and think. Drawing natural objects helps us understand harmony and contrasts and allows us to study form, texture, shape, and motion. This is the language of the designer and is used in every field of design. In academic subjects we make notes; as designers we make notes by drawing, painting, and sketching, slowly building up our language and at the same time gaining experience. Learn this language by drawing as many natural forms as possible. Simplify and reorganise them. You will eventually discover a whole new personal awareness to express in your work.

In this book I have drawn and painted natural objects and shown the designs that can be developed from them. Various graphic techniques have been used, but in some cases I have started off with a photograph of the natural form in order to demonstrate more clearly the progression that takes place from the object under study to the finished article.

Creative design requires a combination of observation and technical skills. Only with this understanding can you bridge the gap between two- and three-dimensional work.

1
Aspects of design

It is necessary to develop our senses to become aware of design and this can only be achieved by seeing and thinking. Time must be spent observing and drawing.

Understanding the language of design is a process that must follow a logical pattern. You must train yourself to concentrate only on one design aspect at a time as there is so much confusing variety in nature. Each natural object has a character of its own that you must try to interpret. Get into the habit of making sketches, if only fragmentary. These sketches are the stepping stones to learning a new language. They will help to establish these shapes in your memory and will be useful for reference purposes when developing a design.

Start a collection of natural forms—leaves, bark, bones, shells, roots, etc. Handle them, feel the different textures, observe the patterns, colours and shapes.

Collect photographs and clippings from magazines, and not only of natural forms. Alongside your technical books have a selection of books on art, sculpture and contemporary design in both domestic and industrial fields.

2
Geometric shapes

All natural forms can be simplified and adapted into geometrical forms. This will be our starting point for study. Using black card or paper, a pair of scissors and a knife, we can cut simple geometric shapes. By producing these shapes with straight or curved cuts we arrive at a whole range of shapes and designs that could be suitable for use in jewellery making, veneering or constructing panels with wood, metal and enamels. Using cut paper to create a design allows you to arrange and rearrange these shapes before arriving at a final decision.

Make a start by cutting several discs 100mm diameter from black card. With a pair of scissors or a knife make one straight cut across one of the discs. Arrange the two pieces on a white card, allowing the white card to show through the gap. When a satisfactory arrangement is reached, paste the pieces into position.

Cut the next disc with two straight cuts, then arrange and paste into position.

Repeat this with the other discs using several straight cuts. Repeat again by using only curved cuts, using one curved cut across a disc, then two cuts and finally make several cuts across a disc.

This can be repeated with other geometric shapes. Extend this still further by introducing grey paper shapes with the black paper shapes.

Illustrated on page 11 are simple pebble forms cut in grey paper with a similar shape cut in black paper. Form the black shapes into areas of design that are in harmony with the grey pebble shapes and paste into position. Coloured gummed paper could be substituted for the black paper.

SUGGESTIONS FOR STUDY

Drawing
Cut several 100mm diameter discs from black card or paper.
1 Make one straight cut across a disc.
2 Make two straight cuts across or into a disc.
3 Make several straight cuts across or into a disc.
4 Make one curved cut across a disc.
5 Make two curved cuts across or into a disc.
6 Make several curved cuts across a disc.
7 Combine straight and curved cuts across a disc.
8 Repeat the above using other geometric forms.
9 Remove one or more pieces of the cut forms.
10 Add one or more pieces in a similar form, using a contrasting colour.
11 Create designs using similar shapes of different sizes.
12 Draw natural objects that have geometric characteristics, e.g., circular forms, cross-sections of stems, branches, seeds.

Practical work

1 Cut geometric shapes from sheet metal, veneer, and plywood. Repeat the exercises used with paper.
2 Combine geometric shapes in plastics sheet with similar shapes in wood and metal.
3 Create designs using metal or veneer strips formed into rings. Use singly or in groups.
4 Create designs by boring and drilling.
5 Create designs using cut sections of tube, bar and dowel.
6 Create designs combining boring, drilling, with tube and dowel.
7 Create free-standing sculptural forms by cutting and interlocking similar shapes together.
8 Create a mobile design using similar geometric shapes in wood, metal, plastics, mirrors.
9 Design jewellery based on geometric forms from natural objects.

Shapes cut from discs of black paper

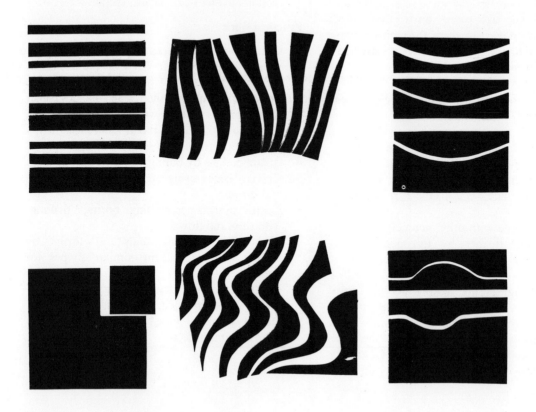

Shapes cut from squares of black paper

Real pebbles . . .

. . . and pebble forms cut from grey and black paper

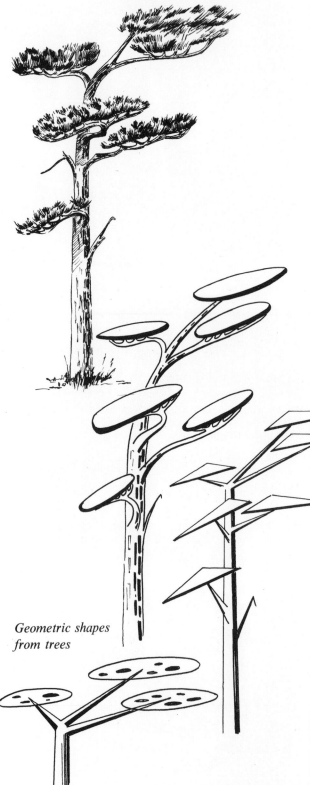

*Geometric shapes
from trees*

Geometric shapes from a cock

3
The line

Our next basic means of graphic expression is the line. With a line the designer can graphically interpret the varying moods of nature, from the undulating lines of water flowing in the stream to the stark, barren silhouette of trees in winter.

We find that nature provides us with straight, curved and angular lines. Each line has a characteristic of its own that must be carefully observed and drawn. Lines can vary from thin, thick, thick to thin, thin to thick. The lines of the thistle are sharp and angular, whereas the lines of a tree root are sinuous, curved and flowing. We see lines that radiate as in a feather, or form surface patterns; lines that enclose forms, or lines that enclose space between the forms. Study nature closely, think, then draw.

SUGGESTIONS FOR STUDY

Drawing

1 Draw various types of line using pencil, pen and ink, nylon-tipped pen, brush, crayon.
2 Draw various types of natural objects using only a line.
3 Make continuous line drawings of natural objects.
4 Draw in perspective using one vanishing point.
5 Create designs using strips of black paper on white card.
6 Create designs using strips of coloured paper or strips cut from coloured magazines.
7 Paint the surface of the paper with a mixture of poster paint and cellulose adhesive. Create linear design in this surface using the end of a brush, fingers, etc.
8 Rub black wax crayon on the paper surface. Crayon over with coloured crayons. Scratch lines through the top colour.
9 Create linear designs in lino and make prints.
10 Create designs with string; glue onto stiff card.

Practical work

Create designs using only curved lines.
Create designs using only straight lines.
Create designs using only angular lines.
Create designs using only radiating lines.

1 Design a panel using various lengths, widths and types of wood.
2 Create designs using veneer strips. Glue face down or form curves and arrange in groups.
3 Create designs using a plough plane, paint the ploughed lines with poster paint, or insert strips of wood or plywood.
4 Create designs using a tenon saw, inserting strips of veneer. These could be allowed to project above the surface.
5 Create designs using various lengths and sizes of dowel. These could be cut square or at an angle.
6 Create designs by accentuating the grain in wood with the use of a vee tool. These could be left plain or filled with coloured wax and the surface cleaned up.
7 Create designs using metal strips, used as flat or curved forms. Rivet or solder together, combine different metals.
8 Create linear designs by forging, welding and brazing, using round, square or flat bars.
9 Create linear designs in sheet metal by etching; these could be used for making prints.
10 Create linear designs with enamel, using enamel threads, sgraffito, cloisonné and champlevé techniques.
11 Create designs by combining enamels, metals and wood.
12 Create designs by scribing lines into transparent plastic sheet. These could be formed into curves and be free-standing.
13 Create linear designs by hammering panel pins into a panel and stretching cotton or Lurex thread between the pins.
14 Create linear designs using fluorescent plastics strips glued into ploughed wood.
15 Design free-standing linear sculpture by interlocking and gluing strips of wood, metal and plastics.
16 Create spatial linear sculpture by bending 1m of 4mm round or square bar at right angles.

Lines in nature

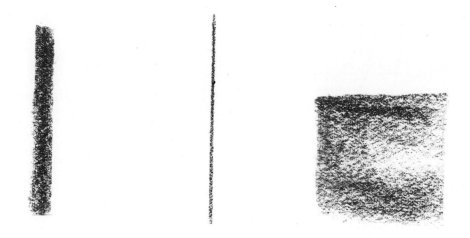

Lines drawn with a square Conté crayon

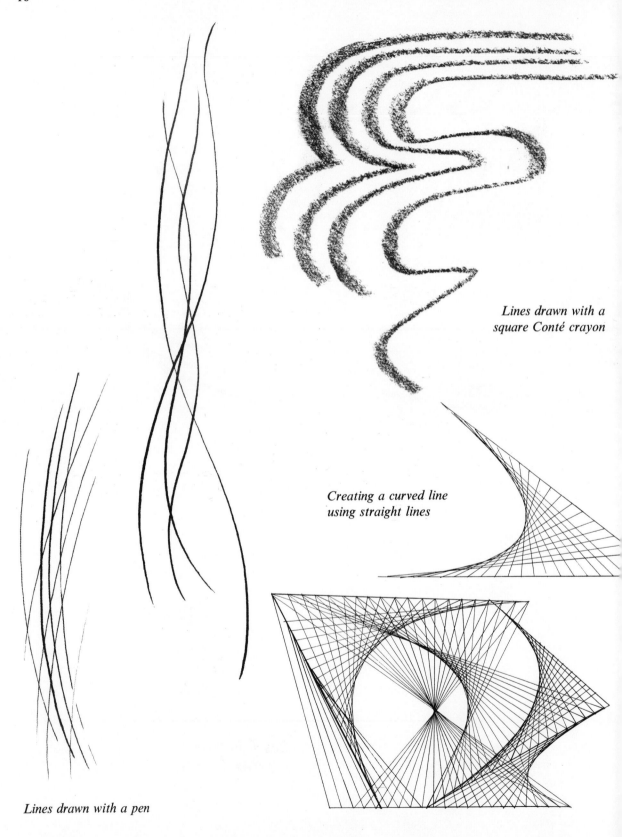

*Lines drawn with a
square Conté crayon*

*Creating a curved line
using straight lines*

Lines drawn with a pen

Drawing with a continuous line

4
Graphic media

Illustrated in the next few pages is a variety of graphic media other than pencil that can be used in creating designs. A square crayon such as a Conté can give variety of lines and tones; pen and ink gives a dense black line and the flexibility of the nib gives expression to the line. Brush and watercolour is a versatile graphic medium. It can be used for laying a wash of flat colour or a gradated wash, used almost dry to give texture, rolled, twisted to create pattern and finally for a whole range of brush lines. A modern nylon-tipped pen is an ideal instrument for drawing a dense line and areas of tone can be quickly formed by washing clean water over the drawing.

Another method of creating a line combined with wash is by the use of greaseproof paper. Lay the greaseproof paper on the drawing paper then, using a pencil or the end of a brush, draw a linear design. Remove the greaseproof paper and wash over with colour.

Also illustrated are several techniques that can be used to represent a range of materials used in the craft rooms. Three stages are needed to portray a flat polished surface such as a coffee table. Start with a flat wash, dry your brush then bring it across the wet wash once or twice to give highlights or reflected light. Allow this wash to dry, then brush on a broken darker wash, keeping the nearest edge darker.

Lines and textures can be created by using a penknife to scratch a dry wash, or areas may be masked off by means of Sellotape prior to washing over with colour, removing the tape when the wash has dried.

SUGGESTIONS FOR STUDY

1 Make wash drawings of simple natural forms such as shells, pebbles or leaves, using one tone of colour, ignoring pattern.
2 Using waterproof ink make a pen drawing and wash over with colour.
3 Draw a few rectangles and cylindrical shapes, with washes to represent various materials.
4 Create designs for jewellery using wax resist and wash.
5 Make wash drawings of a variety of natural objects, each with a different texture.
6 Make wash drawings of natural objects using a tonal scale of five washes.

Three stages in making a wash drawing of a glass beaker

Use line to represent glass

Use wax resist and wash to represent rough casting

Use wash to represent mild steel

Use wash to represent a satin finish on metal

Use wash to represent a highly polished metal surface

Use broken wash to represent wood

Drawing with a dot

My illustrations were drawn on white card using pen and ink. A nylon-tipped pen on cartridge paper would be suitable for this type of drawing. Use the pen gently to avoid spreading the tip. Make a light pencil drawing first and start to shade the drawing with the point of the pen. Do not use a line, only dots. This type of drawing is a slow process and its value is in allowing you time to observe and slowly build up the form.

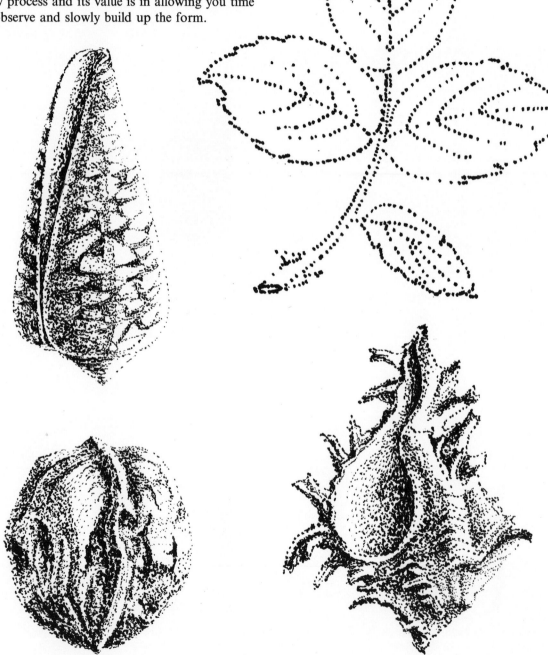

Nylon-tipped pen and wash

This technique is very good for making quick sketches with tone and as an introduction to wash drawing. Draw the object with a nylon-tipped pen then, using clean water, wash over those parts of the drawing requiring tone. The water combines with the ink giving a wash of colour; the density of the colour depending on the amount of pen work.

Wax resist

Textures can be formed by the use of a wax resist. Rub a wax candle on the required area and wash over with watercolour, which will run away from the wax.

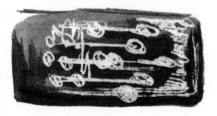

Wash drawing

Before commencing wash for the first time, I suggest you draw a panel divided into six sections. Mix your watercolour in a palette, making five washes of colour ranging from light to dark. Test these washes on a piece of scrap paper until you arrive at the desired range of tones. Paint the panel with clean water and allow it to become damp/dry. This could be hastened by using a piece of blotting paper to absorb excess water. Take a large brush, dip into your lightest tone and begin to paint over five sections, starting along the top edge and brushing your colour from the top to the bottom edge of the panel. At all times keep the bottom edge of the wash fluid; do not allow it to dry. When you have reached the bottom edge, brush the colour to a corner, dry your brush and absorb the surplus wash by touching with the dry brush. Allow this wash to dry then paint over four sections with the next tone, repeating the process again for the remaining sections.

Now that you have made a tonal scale start on your drawing. This should be drawn lightly in pencil, following the procedure used in painting the panel, beginning with your lightest tone and gradually working to the darkest tone.

There are several methods of wash drawing. It is possible to wash a light tone on the drawing and work in the darkest tone while it is still wet. This technique requires practice in observation and skill and I would not recommend it for a beginner. Like most skills wash drawing requires practice and with this your drawing will eventually acquire a personal character.

Hints on wash drawing

Mix your colour thoroughly.

Make tests on scrap paper to ensure an even tonal scale.

Always use as large a brush as possible.

Allow each wash to dry before placing the next wash.

For large wash drawings immerse the paper in water, drain off the surplus water and tape down the edges of the paper onto a board, allowing it to dry and then stretch.

For small wash drawings it is sufficient to paint the drawing only, using clean water.

Stages in making a wash drawing of a ring

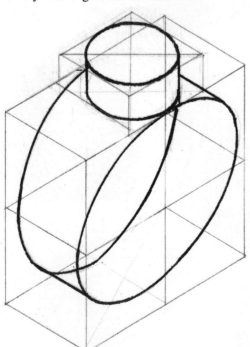

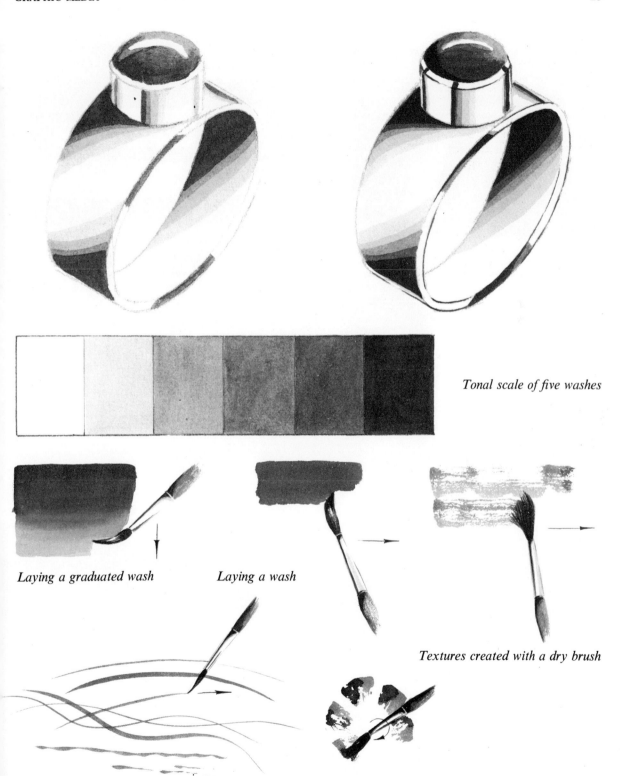

Tonal scale of five washes

Laying a graduated wash

Laying a wash

Textures created with a dry brush

A variety of lines drawn with a brush

Pattern and texture created by rolling a brush

*Areas masked off with Sellotape prior to
washing over with colour*

*Lines and textures created by scratching a dry
wash with a penknife*

5
Pattern and texture

The world would be a very dull place without textures or pattern. Just imagine everything smooth and plain with no sensation to the touch of your fingers and no stimulation for the eyes. Fortunately for us we have an abundance of textures and pattern—so many that we have to be selective.

Take a look at nature. Look at the whole landscape and then look at the individual items that make up the mass. The shell picked up from the beach, a leaf, the bark on the trees. Are they rough or smooth to touch? Look at the pattern on the shell, the discolouration of the leaf, the texture of the bark. Collect various natural textures and patterns, putting them into categories: smooth, rough, soft, linear, dot, multi-unit, transparent, opaque. Draw them full size or just draw a small section, enlarging it as though under a magnifying glass. An aid to visual selection of pattern in natural objects is the use of strips of adhesive paper made into a frame and stuck around areas to isolate them.

To convert an object that is three-dimensional into a two-dimensional image it is necessary to look at the mass as though it were a flat plane without depth. Try and imagine its being put under a roller and flattened.

Make a start by supporting a natural object in a base of modelling clay and directing a light on it from an adjustable table lamp. Pin a piece of grey or black paper on a board and place behind the object. Lightly trace around the shadow thrown on the paper and cut it out with a pair of scissors or a knife. A variety of shapes can be found by turning the object on its axis. The three patterns of rose leaves on page 29 were created by turning the spray through 90°. Other shapes illustrated

are of shells, bones and plant forms. Remember that the cut shapes can be cut into smaller pieces to create more designs.

The shapes can be combined with areas of colour and line to create patterns. The designs from a small tree root shown on page 31 were made by cutting the shadow shape from grey paper and adding pattern with black paint, then painting the root shape in grey poster paint, adding a continuous line for pattern.

With the thistle design on page 32 a brush drawing was made in grey poster paint then over-painted with black poster paint. A further extension of this technique is the panel on page 32 where the design is based on the sharp angular shape of the thistle leaf, using grey and black poster paint with the areas of white. The illustration on page 33 shows a detailed pen and ink drawing combined with wash of a design created from a piece of driftwood.

SUGGESTIONS FOR STUDY

Drawing

1 Divide your paper into areas and using a pen or pencil draw various textures from natural objects.
2 Create your own textures using wax resist, dry brush technique and splattering or dripping watercolour.
3 Create design by painting your paper with clean water and dropping watercolour or ink onto it.
4 Create textures by painting areas with PVA adhesive and sprinkling sawdust, sand, etc., on them.
5 Take black wax rubbings of bark, leaves, etc.
6 Make shadow papercuts from natural objects, using black or grey paper.
7 Create patterns with similar units cut from card or the pages of coloured magazines.
8 Combine these units with line.
9 Isolate areas of pattern and texture on natural objects and enlarge, developing designs from them.

Practical work

1 Create textures by cutting the surface of wood and metal using drills, saws, gouges or files.
2 Create texture by burning the surface of wood and brushing with a wire brush.
3 Create texture by combining sections of wood, using end-grain with the face side.
4 Create a design using cubes of wood, cutting one or more sides at an angle and gluing together to form a panel.
5 Make a texture-board using as many various textures as can be found in the workshop, i.e., shavings, sawdust, etc.
6 Create textures by melting the surface of sheet copper or nickel silver and gilding metal with a brazing torch.
7 Create patterns by smelting copper wire and brazing rod with a brazing torch.
8 Create textures by etching metals.
9 Create textures by beating and punching metal.
10 Create pattern by combining various types and thicknesses of metal and mounting on wood.
11 Create texture by underfiring enamel.
12 Create pattern by combining opaque and transparent enamels.
13 Create patterns by using similar units, i.e., metal washers, springs or nuts and bolts.
14 Create textures by casting, using patterns made from wood, clay, wax, or expanded polystyrene.
15 Design free-standing sculpture by combining similar units, i.e., paper clips, machine nuts or springs.
16 Create jewellery by combining similar units, i.e., sections of tube, rings or chain.

Patterns from natural forms

Agate slab

Shell

Cowrie shell

Lotus pod

Sea urchin

Timber knot

Leaf

Shell

Bark

Peacock feather

Fur

Wool

Mexican agate

Sponge

Stone

Feather

Shell

Shell

Brush drawings based on plant forms

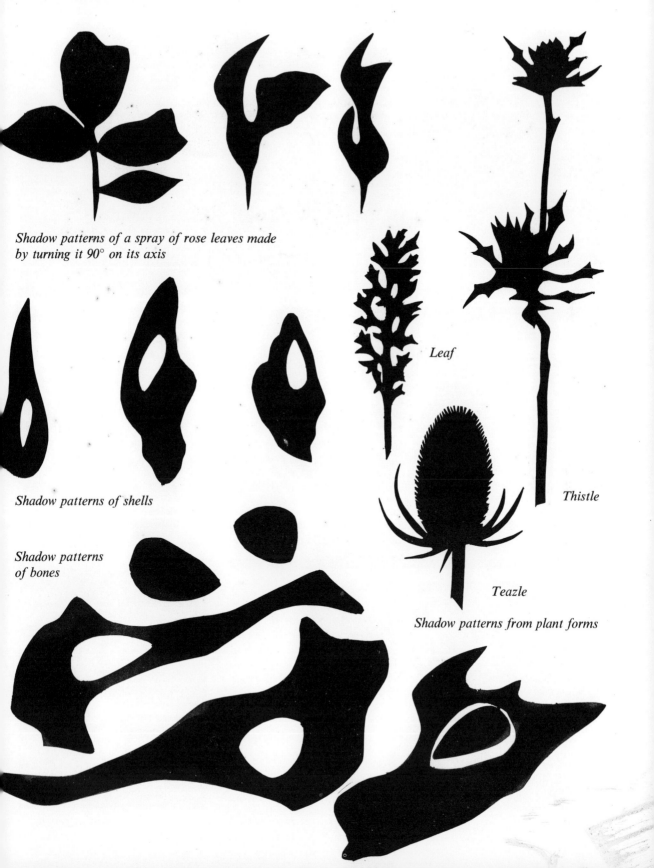

Shadow patterns of a spray of rose leaves made
by turning it 90° on its axis

Leaf

Shadow patterns of shells

Shadow patterns
of bones

Thistle

Teazle

Shadow patterns from plant forms

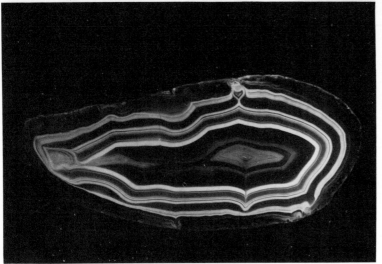

An agate

*The design created
from an agate*

*Isolating areas of pattern and texture on pebbles
and enlarging to create design*

Shadow pattern of a root in grey paper with added pattern in black poster paint

Wash drawing of a root combined with a continuous line

Brush drawing of a thistle in grey and black poster paint

Design in grey and black based on a thistle leaf

*Pattern based on a
piece of driftwood*

6 Three-dimensional representation

Now we arrive at the stage of representing nature in three dimensions. This means you must look at the natural object and within the limits of a flat plane convey the impression of a third dimension. You have drawn lines that have formed boundaries and arrived at a shape. This shape now requires light and shade to emphasise the form and give it depth.

Start with a simple natural object and direct a light from one source on to the form. An adjustable table lamp is ideal for this purpose. Should you find difficulty in supporting the object for study, try making a base from modelling clay. Now you have a light shining on the object from one side, this side will have the lightest tone. There will be a gradation of tone until you reach the opposite side which will be in shadow.

The technique of representing three dimensions requires not only skill in using graphic media, but also an understanding of the form. Look carefully at the object you are going to draw. Is it sharp and angular or round and smooth? Has it a textured surface?

Do not be discouraged by your first attempt. If you have spent half an hour or more drawing a natural object you may not have a masterpiece, but you will have a deeper understanding of that object by simply having observed it closely for a period of time.

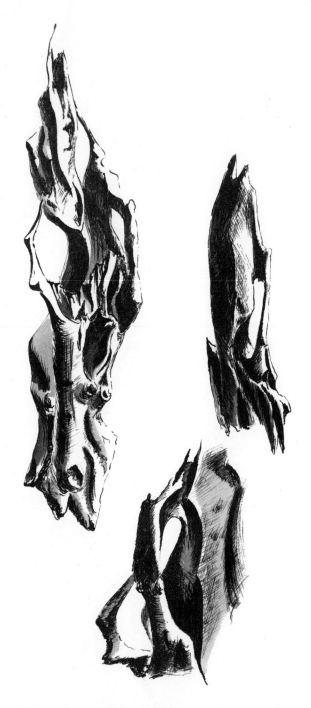

Three-dimensional representation of a piece of driftwood

7
Adapting natural form into pattern and sculptural form

One must have a starting point for design. This may be a drawing direct from nature or it could be a photograph of a natural form taken from a book or magazine. Illustrated are a selection of natural forms showing how they can be adapted into designs—by simplification into line drawings, patterns and sculptural forms—while at the same time keeping their recognisable forms.

If you cannot begin work with the actual object, always try to start with a photograph of what you are going to use as a basis for your design
Both photographs by courtesy of Bruce Coleman Ltd

Panel in 6mm mild steel square bar with enamel

Make an accurate drawing and carry on from there

Ashtray in champlevé enamel

Cloisonné enamel

Cloisonné enamel   *Mosaic enamel*   *Champlevé enamel*

Wood carving with wire legs

Tibetan yak
By courtesy of Bruce Coleman Ltd

Simple wood carvings. Horns are subsequently
made from wood dowel or stainless steel rod

Welded sculptural form based on a vulture

Panel from 6mm and 4mm mild steel bar with applied enamels

Lotus pod

Cast silver pendant

Pendant

Wood carving

Holly leaves

Wood carving designs based on seed forms

Designs for wood carvings

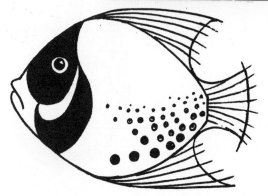

Mosaic with enamel wire

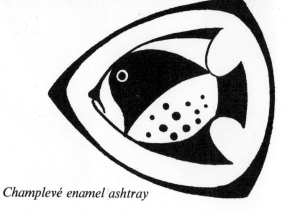

Champlevé enamel ashtray

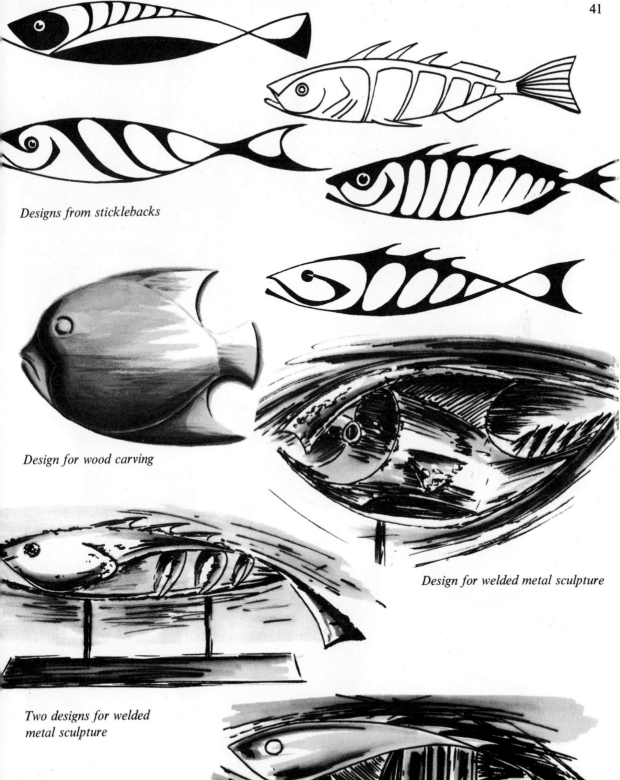

Designs from sticklebacks

Design for wood carving

Design for welded metal sculpture

Two designs for welded metal sculpture

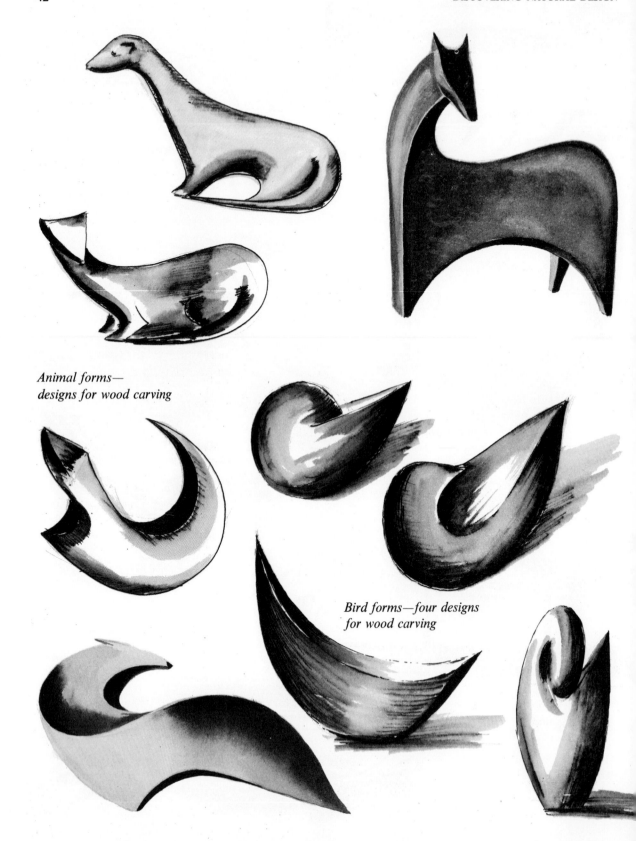

*Animal forms—
designs for wood carving*

*Bird forms—four designs
for wood carving*

8
Abstract forms from nature

This section of illustrations shows how natural forms used as a starting point can be adapted to create abstract shapes and sculptural forms.

It is only when one isolates something from its environment that its design can be really appreciated. Looking at the surface reveals how the pattern and texture is related to the form. Seashell forms, for example, can be transformed into sculpture that will have a feeling of marine life, although not representing any particular shell.

This also applies to the study and drawing of bones, nature's most perfect forms. It will be seen that the sculptural qualities of bones can be freely adapted into sculptural forms.

The human form has been a source of artistic inspiration since primitive man recorded his surroundings and achievements on cave walls, and over the years there have been many interpretations of the human form in works of art.

The starting point for the abstract designs on pages 48–9 were based on a photograph of college students studying the art of movement. By using a fluid line-drawing to indicate the main body-lines of movement, we arrive at a two-dimensional pattern of this movement. These directional lines of movement can also be used as a basis for creating abstract sculptural forms.

Wash drawings of shells

Wood carvings based on shell forms

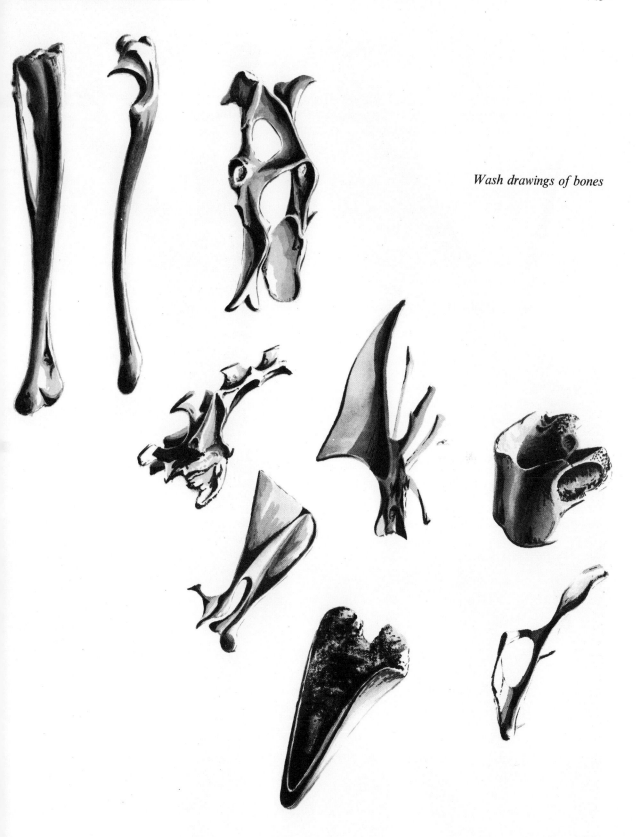

Wash drawings of bones

46

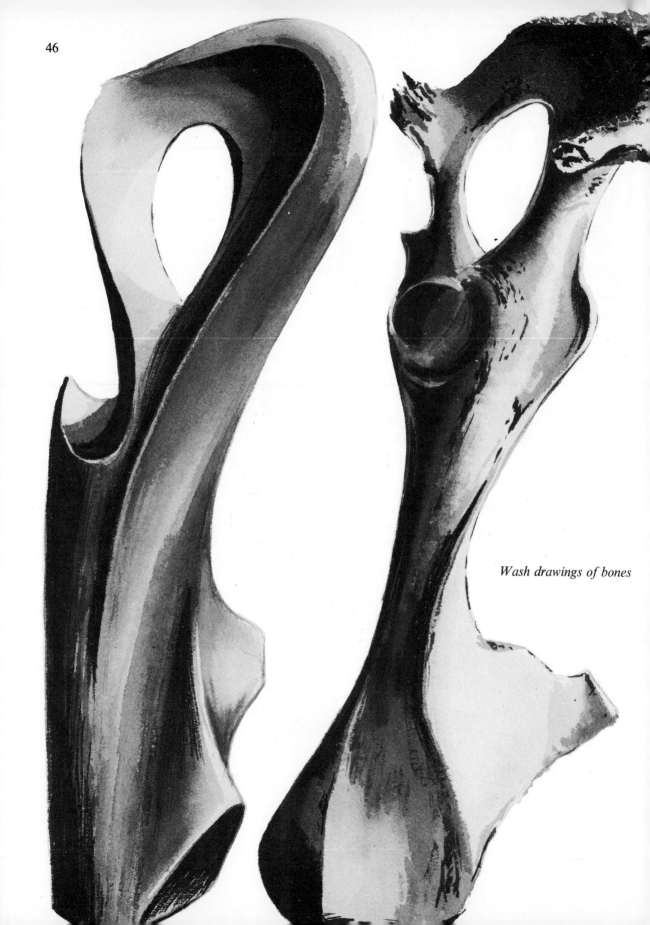

Wash drawings of bones

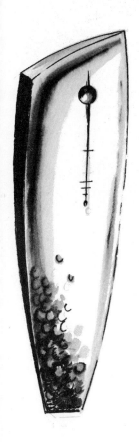

Forged brass sculpture designs based on bone forms

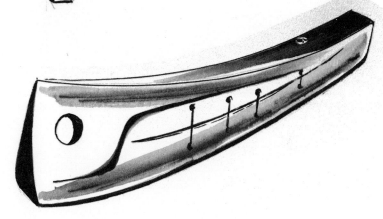

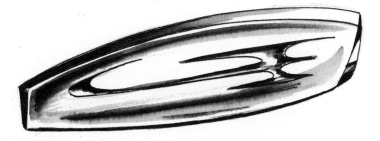

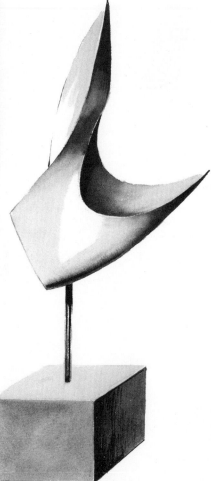

Wood carving design based on human forms in movement

Designs based on human forms in movement

Metal sculpture designs based on human forms in movement

9 Microscopy

With the use of a microscope or micro-projector it is now possible to open up another field of design. Under a microscope there is an infinite variety of shape, colour and cellular structure that would be invisible to the naked eye. The use of this extends the designer's brief, and in most areas of design we have become familiar with shapes that have been inspired by the use of the microscope.

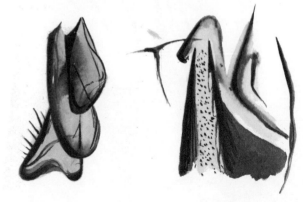

Parts of a gnat greatly magnified

Worker bee mouth and tongue magnified 10 × 10

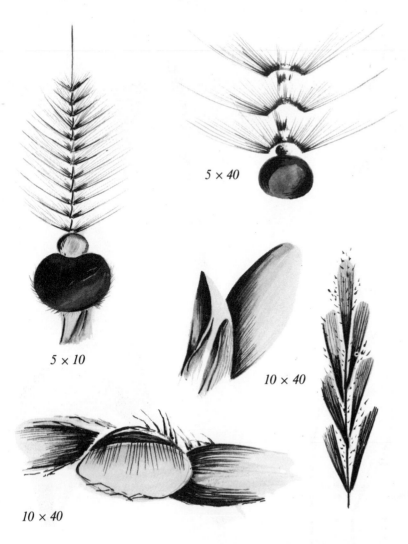

5 × 40

5 × 10

10 × 40

10 × 40

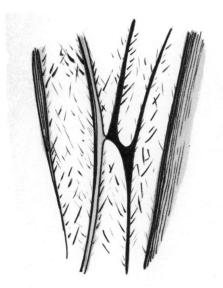

Beetle spiracle (aperture for breathing) magnified 10 × 10

Wasp wing magnified 10 × 10

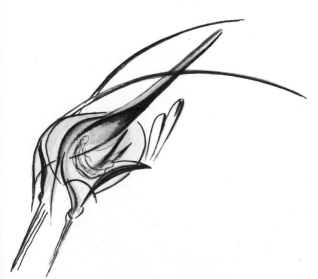

Wasp mouth parts magnified 5 × 10

Wasp sting and poison sac magnified 5 × 4

Jaws of nereis (carnivorous marine worm) magnified 5 × 10

Pollen grains magnified 15 × 10

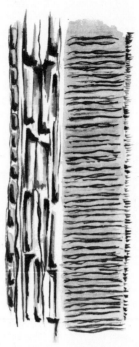

Marrow stem sieve tubes magnified 15 × 10

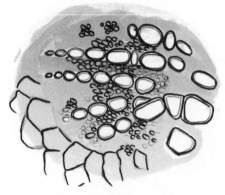

Helianthus stem magnified 15 × 10

*Tulip leaf epidermis stomata
(microscopic openings for gaseous
exchange) magnified 15 × 10*

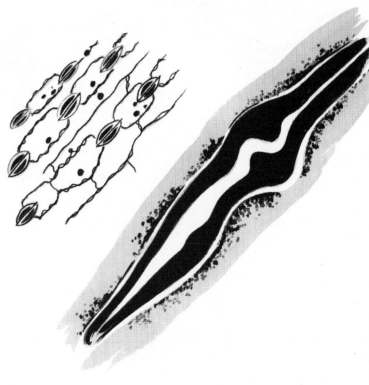

Marrow sieve tubes magnified 15 × 10

10
Jewellery

During the last few years there has been an increase in the designing and making of jewellery. With the availability of lapidary equipment and materials it is within the reach of most of us to cut and polish our own semi-precious stones. This last section is devoted to the designing of jewellery suitable for making in the school workshop.

Illustrated are a few minute marine forms called plankton. These were drawn with pen and ink and then washed over with coloured inks. Several sketches of jewellery shapes were evolved from these pen and ink drawings, adapting the plankton shapes into a practical form. Selected designs were then drawn with white poster paint on black cartridge paper.

Designs for jewellery can be developed from most natural forms, and illustrated on the next few pages are some based on a simple fish form. The first few designs resemble a fish, but eventually we can lose the fish yet still keep the basic shape and movement, and develop a whole range of related designs.

Another approach to designing jewellery is by the drawing of geometrical and symmetrical shapes, and within the confines of these simple shapes developing our own designs.

The final drawings are of rings with cabochon-cut stones. These were drawn in both wash and opaque poster paint on grey mounting board.

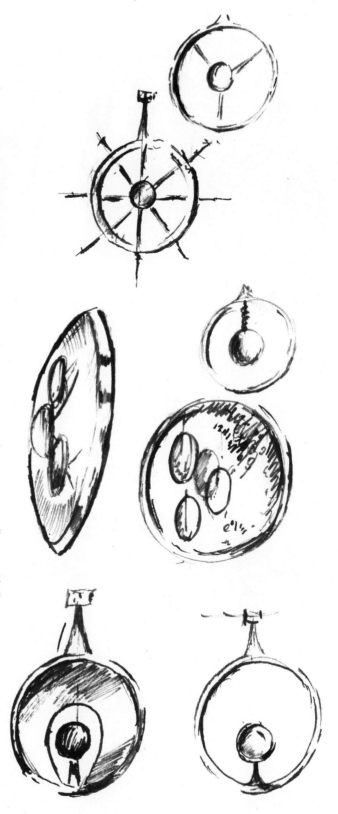

Jewellery forms based on plankton

Designs for jewellery based on a fish form

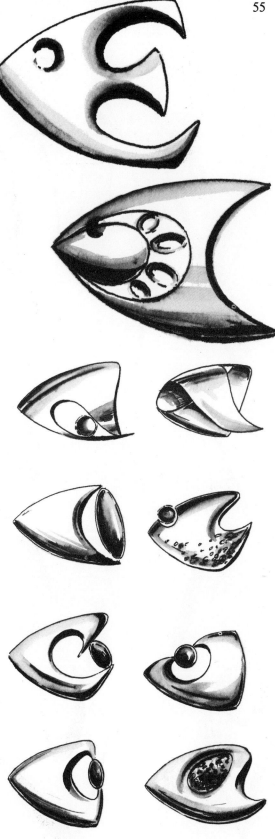

Jewellery designs based on symmetrical forms

Jewellery designs based on geometrical forms

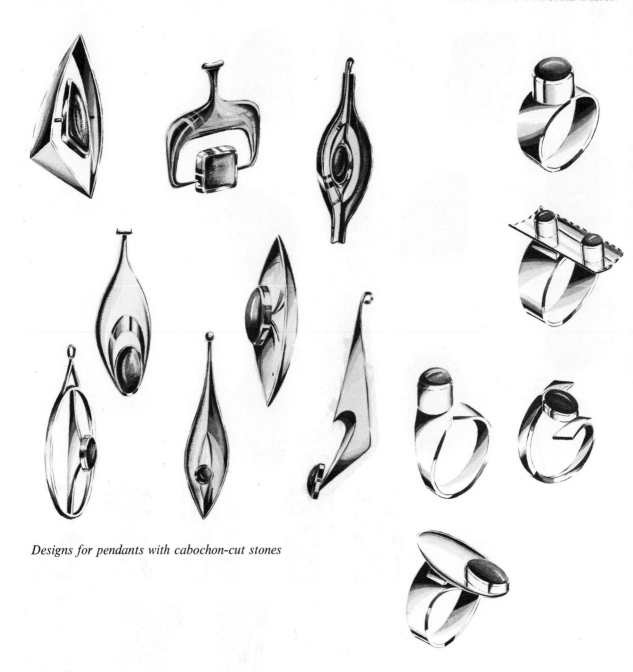

Designs for pendants with cabochon-cut stones

Designs for rings with cabochon-cut stones

Designs for rings with cabochon-cut stones

11
Author's work

Bird form, height 300mm
Bronze welded brass sheet

Fighting cocks, height 350mm
Mahogany

Yak
Carving

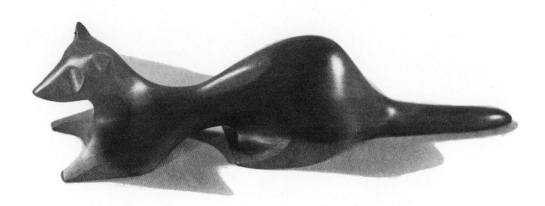

Animal form, length 300mm
Mahogany

Hedgehogs

Ram and hippo

Bull, length 600mm
Sycamore

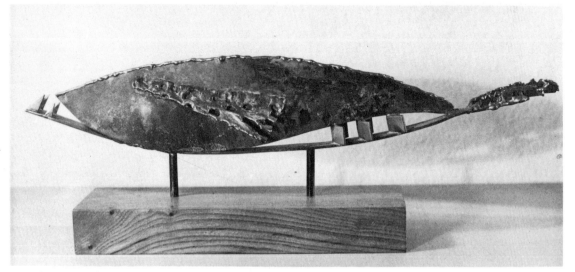

Fish form, length 500mm
Bronze welded brass sheet

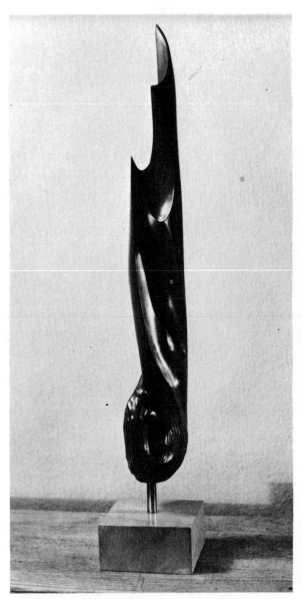

Plant form, height 600mm
Mahogany

Plant form, height 450mm
Bronze welded brass sheet

Bone form, height 750mm
Yew

Bone form, height 450mm
Yew

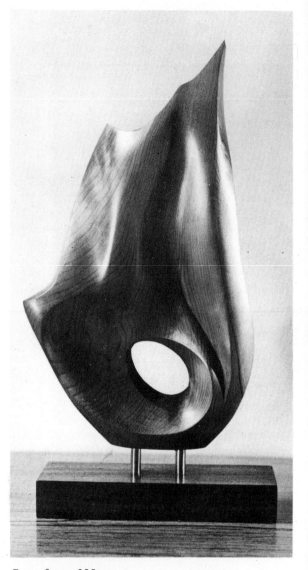

Bone form, height 375mm
Yew

Bone form, 325mm
Yew

Marine form, length 900mm

Shoal of fish, length 900mm
Mahogany

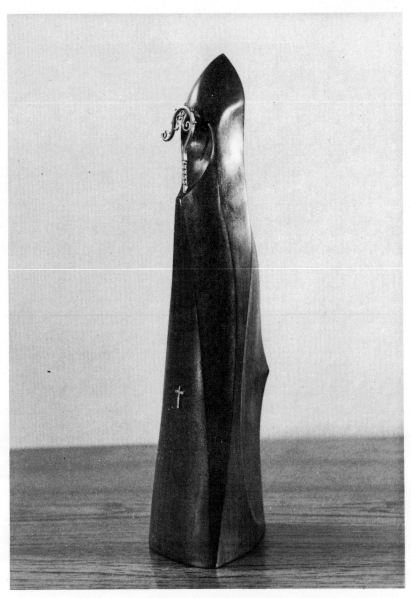

Bishop, height 350mm   Mahogany and silver

Draw knife sculpture, height 1200mm

Pebble forms

Brush designs from natural forms

Bibliography

DESIGN

Form in Nature and Life, Andreas Feininger
  (Thames & Hudson).
Forms and Patterns in Nature, Wolf Strache
  (Peter Owen).
Nature as Designer, Bertel Bager (Warne & Co).
Vision in Motion, L Moholy-Nagy (Paul Theobold,
  Chicago).
Constructivism, George Rickey (Studio Vista).
Looking and Seeing Series, Kurt Rowland (Ginn
  & Co).
The Nature of Design, David Pye (Studio Vista).

JEWELLERY MAKING

The Design and Creation of Jewellery, Robert Von
  Neumann (Pitman).
Contemporary Jewellery, Philip Morton (Holt
  Rinehart & Winston Inc, London).
Handwrought Jewellery, L E Franke and W L
  Udell (McKnight & McKnight, USA).
Creative Casting, Sharr Choate (Allen & Unwin).
Jewellery and Sculpture Through Unit Construction,
  Patricia Meyerowitz (Studio Vista).
Lost Wax Casting of Jewellery, Keith Edwards
  (Mills & Boon).

LAPIDARY WORK

Discovering Lapidary Work, John Wainwright
  (Mills & Boon).
Gem Cutting, John Sinkankas (Van Nostrand
  Reinhold).

ENAMELLING

The Craft of Enamelling, Kenneth Neville (Mills
  & Boon).
Enamelling Jewellery Work, Brian Newble (Studio
  Vista).
Enamelling on Metal, Oppi Untracht (Pitman).

METAL SCULPTURE

Direct Metal Sculpture, Dona Meilach and D
  Seiden (Allen & Unwin).
Metal Sculpture, John Lynch (Studio Vista).

WOOD SCULPTURE

Foundation of Design in Wood, Francis Zanker
  (Dryad Press).
Wood Sculpture, R Cartmell (Mills & Boon).
Creative Wood Craft, Ernst Rottger (Batsford).
Barbara Hepworth, J P Hodin (Lund Humphries).

PLASTICS

Plastics for Schools, Peter J Clarke (Mills & Boon).
Plastics as an Art Form, Thelma Newman
  (Pitman).

PAPER

New Dimensions in Paper Craft, Samadi Yamada
  and Ito Kiyotada (Pitman).
Creative Paper Craft, Ernst Rottger (Batsford).

Materials
and suppliers

MATERIALS	SUPPLIERS
Enamels and sundry equipment	W G Ball Ltd Anchor Road Longton Stoke on Trent
Enamelling kits	Enamelaire 61B High Street Watford Herts
Craft materials	Arts and Crafts Unlimited 49 Shelton Street London WC2
Etching materials	T N Lawrence 2–4 Bleeding Heart Yard Greville Street London EC1
	Cornelissen and Sons Art Colourmen 22 Great Queen Street London WC2
Gold, silver, findings, silver solder, etc	Johnson Matthey & Co Ltd Vittoria Street Birmingham 1
Polishing and finishing materials	W Canning & Co Ltd Great Hampton Street Birmingham 18
Jewellery tools, findings, etc	Charles Cooper 12 Hatton Wall Hatton Garden London EC1
	E Gray & Sons Ltd 12 Clerkenwell Road London EC1
Non-ferrous metals	J Smith & Sons (Clerkenwell) Ltd 50 St John's Square London EC1
	Matbrit 18 Highfield Road Manchester 19
Stainless steels	Alfred Simpson Ltd Victoria Street Openshaw Manchester
	John Cashmore Ltd Great Bridge Tipton Staffs
Metal tube	Le Bas Tube Co Ltd 281–285 Talbot Road Stretford Manchester
Hardwoods (carving)	Irvine & Sellers Ltd Saracens Head Halsall Nr Southport
	Porter (Selby) Ltd Doncaster
	Fitchett & Woolacot Popham Street Nottingham
Veneers	Art Veneers Co Ltd Industrial Estate Mildenhall Suffolk
	E C Young Carpenter's Road London E15
Brush making (monofilaments)	Baldwins Ltd Brush Manufacturers 113 Curzon Street Burnley
Lapidary equipment and materials	Avon Gems Boon Street Eckington Nr Pershore Worcs, WR10 3BL
	Peter Roberts Atholl Road Pitlochry Scotland

MATERIALS	SUPPLIERS
	Gemstones 35 Princess Avenue Hull
Precious and semi-precious stones	Bernard C Lowe & Co Ltd 73–75 Spencer Street Birmingham 18
Plastics and polyesters	Griffin & George Ltd Ealing Road Alperton Middlesex HAQ 1HJ
	Trylon Ltd Thrift St Wollaston Northants
	Imperial Chemical Industries Ltd Plastics Division Bessemer Road Welwyn Garden City Herts
Glass and clear and coloured soda glass	Plowden & Thompson Ltd Dial Glass Works Stourbridge Worcs
Stained and handmade glass	James Hetly & Co Ltd Beresford Avenue Wembley Middlesex
Sculpture tools and requisites	Alec Tiranti Charlotte Street London W1